How to Build a Computer

- The Best Beginner's Guide to Building Your Own PC from Scratch! -

By Douglas L. Miller

Copyright © 2018

Table of Contents

Introduction 5
The Parts 8
    Case 9
    Power Supply 12
    Motherboard 16
        Socket Type 17
        Size 18
        External Ports 19
        Amount of RAM Supported 21
        Number of SATA Ports 22
        Integrated Graphics Card 23
    Processor 25
    RAM 27
    Graphics & Sound Cards 29
    Hard Drive 32
    Optical Drive 35
    Software 36
    Where to Buy the Parts 38
Building Your Computer 39
    Opening the Case 40

Mounting the Motherboard 42

Installing the Processor 45

Installing the RAM 48

Installing the PCI Cards 49

Installing the Hard Drive 51

Installing the Optical Drive 53

Installing the Power Supply 54

Connecting Everything 55

24-Pin Motherboard Cable 56

4-Pin Motherboard Cable 57

6-Pin PCI Cables 57

SATA Power and Data Cables 58

Molex Power Cables 59

Front Panel Connectors 61

Power Switch and LEDs 62

Cable Management 64

Troubleshooting 66

Installing the Operating System 69

Editing the BIOS 69

Installing Windows 72

Installing Your Drivers 74

Installing Updates 76
More Resources..79
Conclusion 81

Introduction

Build your own computer? It's not as hard as you might think. It's a matter of buying and assembling the parts to design and craft the perfect machine for your purposes.

Why build your own computer? Let's think about this a minute.

First of all, you might suppose you can save money by building your own machine. That's not true, unfortunately. At any given level of performance, you can buy a ready-built computer more cheaply than you can build one, especially if you take the time to shop around a bit. That's because the markup on the parts when you buy them retail (as you'll have to do unless you want to build a lot of machines) is considerable. The labor to assemble the computers is, by comparison, a trivial cost, and as competitive as the computer market has become these days, the price of ready-built computers is dropping through the floor. And that's even before you figure in the value of included software and the manufacturer's warranty.

So you won't save money; in fact, you'll end up spending more money. Why do it, then? There are two reasons and they're both good ones.

First, you'll get *exactly* the computer you want. When you buy a pre-made machine, you're buying someone else's idea of what a computer ought to have in it, not your own. (Unless you order your computer custom-built, and in that case you *will* save money by doing it yourself.) Whether you want super graphics capacity for the latest games, built-in wireless internet, a half-dozen ports for printers, or a sound card and speakers capable of being a top-flight stereo system, you can make your computer precisely what you want it to be without any compromises.

Not only will you have exactly the hardware you want, but also exactly the software. Premade computers usually come with software already installed, and that's fine if it's the software you want, but a waste of disk space otherwise. What if you don't want the latest edition of Windows but would prefer to run Linux? What if you have a favorite office software suite and aren't interested in Microsoft Office? And why clutter up your computer with silly dinky games you'll never play?

The other reason is that you will, by building your computer, learn how to do that. In learning how to build a computer, you'll also learn how to upgrade one. As fast as the world of computing is changing, as fast as new technological advances render machines obsolete, the ability to open up your computer and install more memory, a bigger hard drive, a faster processor, or an upgraded graphics card is a useful skill. It isn't a very hard skill to learn, but it does take a little application, and there's no better way to motivate yourself to learn it than by building your own dream machine right from the parts.

This e-book will help you do that. You'll find out how to shop for parts, what you'll need to put them together, and how to wire this to that and make your machine come alive.

The Parts

The first thing you need to do is decide what parts you want and find and buy them. This will determine what your machine will be able to do when you're finished with it.

In addition to reading this guide, we recommend that you check out the stats on some pre-built systems in the general category you're looking for: low-end, medium, or high-end; graphics-oriented, sound-oriented, etc. All of the specifics presented here will become obsolete before much time has passed – possibly even before you read this. However, the general concepts will almost certainly still be valid for a considerable time to come.

Case

The case is the outside of the computer. It's important to match the case to the parts that you want to go inside it. Most importantly, match the case to the motherboard in terms of its size. You can find the size of the motherboard in the stats for that device (micro, mini, or full). If you get a case that's bigger than your motherboard calls for, that's not a big problem except that you're wasting space. If you get one that's too small, then it probably won't work.

Other considerations for the computer case are:

- How good is the internal cooling and airflow? How many fans does it have?
- How noisy is it? (This is often the downside of having a lot of fans.)
- How many drive bays does it have? All computer boxes today have at least two drive bays, one for a hard drive and the other for an optical drive. If you want more than this, you need to get a box with more than two drive bays.
- How many ports does it have and where are they located? Ports are built-in connections for USB access, speakers, headphones and microphones, FireWire, and so on. All boxes have at least a few of these in the front. How many do you think you'll use?
- What does it offer for managing your cables? There's an awful lot of wiring inside a computer and if it's not organized and positioned well, you can block the air flow and risk your computer overheating. Some cases have holes built into them for routing

- cables while others leave it up to you to handle everything with twist ties and such.
- How does it look? Remember, you're going to see mostly the outside of your computer every time you use it (along with the monitor screen, of course).

It's a good idea to look for customer reviews on any brand of computer case you're considering. That's the best way to answer most of these questions, and the only way to answer some of them.

Power Supply

This is one piece of hardware that you don't want to cut corners on. The power supply is one of the most common elements of a computer system to fail, although not quite as common as the hard drive. The best thing to do is to choose a top brand and consider the defining features of your power supply.

Wattage: Here's the most obvious thing to consider. How much power do you need for all the things you want to power up? A nice online calculator for necessary wattage for your computer system may be found on this website. It's actually a good idea to overdo the wattage a bit, say by about 100 watts. That leaves you some room for upgrades. Remember, you're not skimping on the power supply, so replacing it when you upgrade is not an ideal way to go.

Noise: The power supply, along with the cooling fans, is a major contributor to the noise your machine generates. Here's a good use for reviews. Check which power supplies are reported as noisier and which ones quieter.

Efficiency: What your power supply does is to take AC current from your wall socket and convert it into a form your computer can use. When that happens, you always lose some power. No power supply has 100% efficiency, and none ever will, because that's physically impossible. Some are more efficient than others, though. More efficient power supplies tend to be quieter for a given wattage and, of course, cost less in electricity to run.

Cables: You need to connect your power supply to all the pieces and parts of your computer that make use of the power. This takes cables, and so all power supplies have cables attached to them. You want long ones that can reach your devices wherever they are located in your case. It's also a plus to have modular cables (ones that detach from the power supply), so that you can include only the ones you need and not have your case cluttered up with cables that don't go anywhere.

Uninterruptable power supply (UPS): This is essentially a battery that runs your computer in the event of a power failure. The idea is to let you do a controlled shut-down if you lose power so that you don't also lose data. Some power supplies have these built in. It's optional, but a nice extra that might be worth considering.

There are many good brands of power supply on the market, including Corsair, Seasonic, Zippy, SilenX, Hiper, and others. Look for reviews, and look at the price – aiming for high rather than low, given a power supply that does what you want it to. It isn't always true in every case that you "get what you pay for," but when it comes to computer power supplies it generally is.

Note that a lot of computer cases come with built-in power supplies. Here you have a judgment call, because power supplies purchased separately tend to be a bit better than those built into computer cases.

Motherboard

The motherboard is like the downtown area of your machine. It contains one or more sockets for processors, as well as circuits and ports that connect everything in your computer to everything else. Here are the important things to consider when choosing a motherboard.

Socket Type

The socket type determines what kind of processor you can use with your motherboard. The processor is the single most important piece of equipment you're going to be buying and, along with a few other things like RAM and cards, determines what programs you can effectively run on your computer. It's a good idea to pick the processor first and choose everything else to accommodate it or make full use of its capabilities.

Size

Motherboards generally come in three sizes: Mini ITX, Micro ATX, and Full ATX. The bigger the motherboard, the more advanced features you can use. Your case size will be determined by the size of the motherboard as well.

External Ports

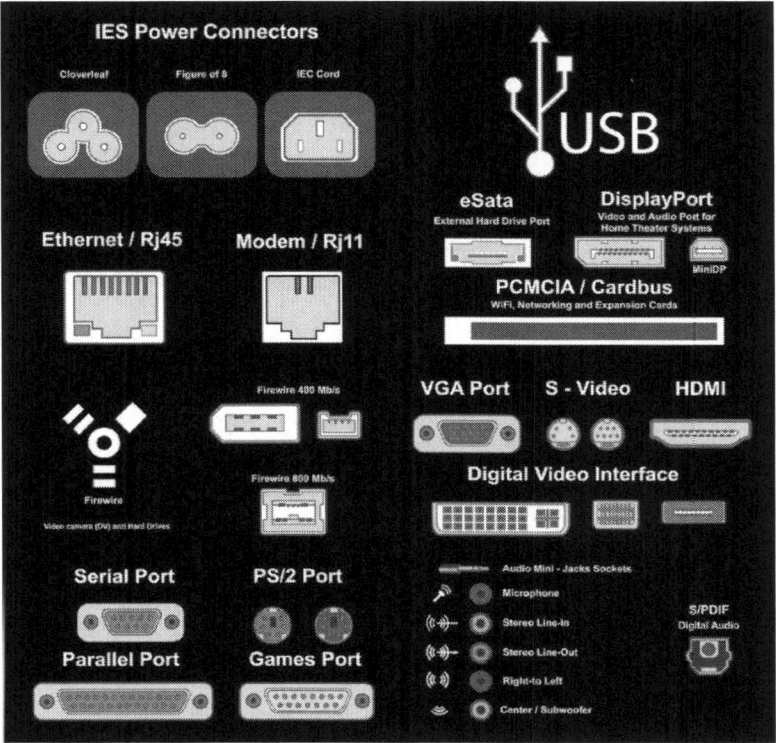

Your motherboard will have a number of ports for external connections. Some of these may be specific (e.g. USB ports) while others may be able to accommodate different types of plug-in cards (e.g. PCI slots). You should have a good idea of how many ports you are going to want to have given what you want your computer to do. As a general rule, the more, the better; if you have ports and slots that you aren't using, that isn't a problem and you may find a use for them later on. Unused ports represent upgrade potential.

Amount of RAM Supported

Two things determine how powerful your machine is and what it is capable of running in terms of software (and at what speed). One of these is the processor speed, and the other is how much RAM it has installed. Your motherboard will have a limit in the amount of RAM it can support. You will want a motherboard that will support all of the RAM you want to install and use (or more).

Number of SATA Ports

This establishes the number of internal hard drives and optical drives you can have. All motherboards support at least one hard drive and one optical drives; many support more than this. This is of concern, of course, only if you plan on using multiple drives.

Integrated Graphics Card

This is a minor point and may or may not be something to look for. Some motherboards have a graphics card built into them. Generally speaking, integrated graphics cards aren't as powerful as the better ones you can buy and install. If you are only going to do things that are at the low end of the graphics scale, then the integrated card available in many motherboards will be just fine. If you plan to play high-end videogames or use other high-end graphics applications, then you'll want a separate card. If you do get a separate card, having an integrated graphics card on your motherboard as well will not hurt anything.

Processor

There are two important variables to look at when buying a processor. These are clock speed and number of cores.

Your processor's clock speed determines the number of instructions a single core can carry out in one second. It represents how fast any one processing core is.

The number of cores tells you how many processes can be going on simultaneously. A single processing core can only do one thing at a time (the appearance of multitasking with a single-core processor is possible because it can switch from one application to another faster than your attention can easily follow). Processors as of this time of writing are available in single, dual, and quad-core. Programs that can use multiple cores at once are especially great for multitasking, and if you want to use such programs, you'll want a dual or quad core processor.

For gaming, clock speed is more important than number of cores, as most videogame software is not written to make use of more than one core. However, that may change in the future.

Most processors come with a cooling fan as part of the package. OEM processors don't, so if you choose a processor with that brand you'll need to buy a separate cooler to go with it. The only real consideration in doing that is to buy one that will work with the processor you choose, and the coolers spell out what they work with up front.

RAM

RAM (Random Access Memory) is a simple concept. The main concern is to make certain that the RAM you choose is compatible with your motherboard. Also, of course you'll want to have enough RAM to do the things you want your computer to do.

RAM is sold in "sticks" that are each four, eight or sixteen GB. Your motherboard will support either dual or triple channels. Dual channels use two sticks, so you'll want to buy RAM in sets of two; triple channels use three, so you'll want to buy it in sets of three sticks.

There's just no reason not to buy the most advanced type of RAM that's sold in electronics stores. Most of it will be that type anyway, with older RAM sold only because some older machines require it. Since you're building a new machine that's not a concern.

One variable to consider is the RAM speed. In fact, RAM speed at this time isn't really a limiting factor for your computer's performance. For almost all purposes, getting the slowest RAM speed available that your motherboard will support (which is usually 1333) is the best approach. (This ceases to be true if you're planning on overclocking your processor.)

Graphics & Sound Cards

As noted above, a lot of motherboards have graphics cards built into them. Just about all motherboards have built-in sound cards. Whether you want to use an external graphics or sound card depends on what you plan to use the computer for.

If you want to play high-end games on your machine, you will definitely want a graphics card. A lot of games are very demanding in terms of graphics card capability. That's also true of high-quality videos. Check the requirements and recommendations for the game or video or graphics software you want to run, and make sure you get a graphics card that meets those recommendations.

As for the sound card, that's a concern mainly if you want to use your computer to play music and want high quality, but even for that, the sound card is less important than the software and the speakers in terms of sound quality. Check the recommendations for the software you want to use.

Hard Drive

There are two measures that are important in deciding on what hard drive to buy. One of these is size. Hard drives are measured in gigabytes of available memory, and obviously you want one that's big enough to store all your programs and data, with room to add more. That said, hard drive upgrades are very cheap these days. You can always add more capacity.

The other measure is hard drive speed. The faster your hard drive is, the faster your programs (including your operating system) will boot and launch, the faster files will open, and (subject to limitations of bandwidth and connection speed) the faster you can download things from the internet. The standard today is 7200 RPM. Some drives will run on serial ATA 3.0 gb/s, but check the SATA ports on your motherboard. If you have 6 gb/s ports, it might be worthwhile to pay a bit more for a SATA 6 gb/s hard drive. (These aren't the actual speeds of data transfer for the drives, by the way.)

Another thing to consider is getting a solid-state drive. These things are very, very fast, but tend to be a bit small, so you probably will need a conventional drive, too. At least, that's the case at the time of this writing. In the future, who knows?

Good brands for standard hard drives are Toshiba, Western Digital, Hitachi, Samsung, and Seagate. For solid-state drives the highest-recommended brands are Intel, Crucial, Corsair, and OCZ.

Optical Drive

In perfect honesty, there isn't a lot of variation for this piece of hardware. They're all read-write drives that burn discs at around the same speed, and all brands on the market are good. The most logical thing to do is to go for whatever you can find on sale.

The one exception is if you're looking for a Blu-Ray drive. In that case the read and write speed does vary, and you'll pay more, naturally, for a faster drive.

Software

In the end, your hardware is only as good as your software – and your software is only as good as your hardware. This is a hugely personal decision, but it determines a lot of your choices in terms of hardware, too.

In terms of operating system, there are three main kinds of personal computers on the market, one of which you can't build yourself anyway (thanks to Apple's closely-held grip on its manufacturing and OS, there's no such thing as building your own Mac), so in practice you have two choices: Windows and Linux. Linux is an open-source operating system, which means you can modify it yourself if you have the skill. It has a good reputation and its adherents totally swear by it.

Windows, whatever its benefits and shortcomings, is by far the more popular operating system, which means that you can find a lot more software applications written to run on it than on Linux. That is the main benefit of using Windows. In addition, you get free updates from Microsoft and access to Microsoft technical support and customer service.

A lot will depend on the answers to two questions. First, how much of a programmer and tinkerer are you? You will need to have some skill and inclination along those lines to get the best benefit from Linux. Second, what software applications do you want to run, and what operating systems are they available to run on? Answer those two questions and the question of what operating system to choose answers itself.

In the process, consider how cool it is that you are able to make that choice instead of having it made for you. If you buy a pre-made computer, it's virtually guaranteed to come with Windows installed.

As for applications software, that's worth a whole book in itself (or many of them). But you should have some idea about that before you spend a single penny on either software or hardware. Build the computer to run the software you want – or a bit more of one – rather than choosing software that will run on your computer.

Where to Buy the Parts

All right, having decided on your shopping list of parts for your new computer, having meticulously planned it all down to the last watt, gigabyte, and processing core, it's finally time to spend some money. Where should you get all this stuff?

In general, the answer is that you should get it where you can get it cheapest. That may be more places than one.

First of all, there's a great online resource for computer components called Newegg.com. You can find most anything there, the prices are reasonable and the service is good. It's wildly popular and you'll hear a lot of good things about it.

However, in point of fact you can often find somewhat better deals at your local electronics stores. So the first thing you should do is to check out Fry's Electronics, Best Buy, or Micro Center. No – that's the second thing you should do. The first thing is to go to Newegg and see what price your parts are going for there. *Then* shop locally and buy anything you can get for a cheaper price. After that, return to Newegg and fill in the remaining gaps.

Building Your Computer

Once you've accumulated all of the parts you need – everything on the list above – you're ready to put your machine together, and for this you need only a couple of tools: a Phillips screwdriver of the right size to work with the screws you'll be screwing, and a sharp knife.

There are three main parts to putting it all together. First, mount and install all of the parts. Second, connect it all together properly. After that, you'll want to run a boot-up test to make sure everything is working. And finally, the last step is to install the operating system.

Opening the Case

The first thing you want to do is to open the case. Take it out of the box, unscrew any screws that are holding it together (set these carefully aside where you can find them for reassembly – they're small and easy to lose), and open it, usually by sliding the side cover off, although this varies a bit from case to case.

Take a look at the case to become familiar with all of its slots and compartments. Note where the bays are for the hard drives, observe where the CD/optical drive will go, where the power supply mounts, and so on. You should also have a bag full of screws inside the case. These are for mounting hardware inside the case; the ones you removed were for fastening the case shut. Remove this bag of screws and set it aside where you can easily find it.

Mounting the Motherboard

Open the motherboard box. You should find two main parts inside. One of these is the motherboard itself, and the other is the I/O shield. This is a metal plate that covers and protects the ports on the back of the case. Snap this into place. It should be obvious where it goes, but a good bit of force is required to snap all four of the connections into place. Make sure all four sides are fastened securely.

Now take the motherboard itself. Line it up with the screw holes on the back of the case. Odds are, you'll have more screw holes on the case than you do on the motherboard, so take careful note of which screw holes on the case are the right ones (you can mark these with magic marker if you want). Make sure the ports on the motherboard line up with the port holes in the back of the case.

Open the bag of screws and take out the motherboard standoffs. These are double screws; that is, they have a male screw that goes into the case screw hole, and then built-in female screw holes for the motherboard screws. Fasten the standoffs into the correct screw holes on the case. Position the motherboard on top of them. Screw the motherboard screws into the standoffs so that the motherboard is securely fastened.

Judgment call time: It may or may not be a good idea to wait on installing the motherboard until after you have the processor installed in the motherboard. It may or may not also be a good idea to install the RAM and power supply first. It's all a matter of which is easier, given the configuration of things with your particular computer. The main goal here is to avoid bumping into anything previous installed and possibly damaging it. Take a look at your equipment, visualize where it should all go, and decide one way or the other; unfortunately there's no way to provide a one-size-fits-all solution. A well-designed case will allow all of this to be done safely in any order.

Installing the Processor

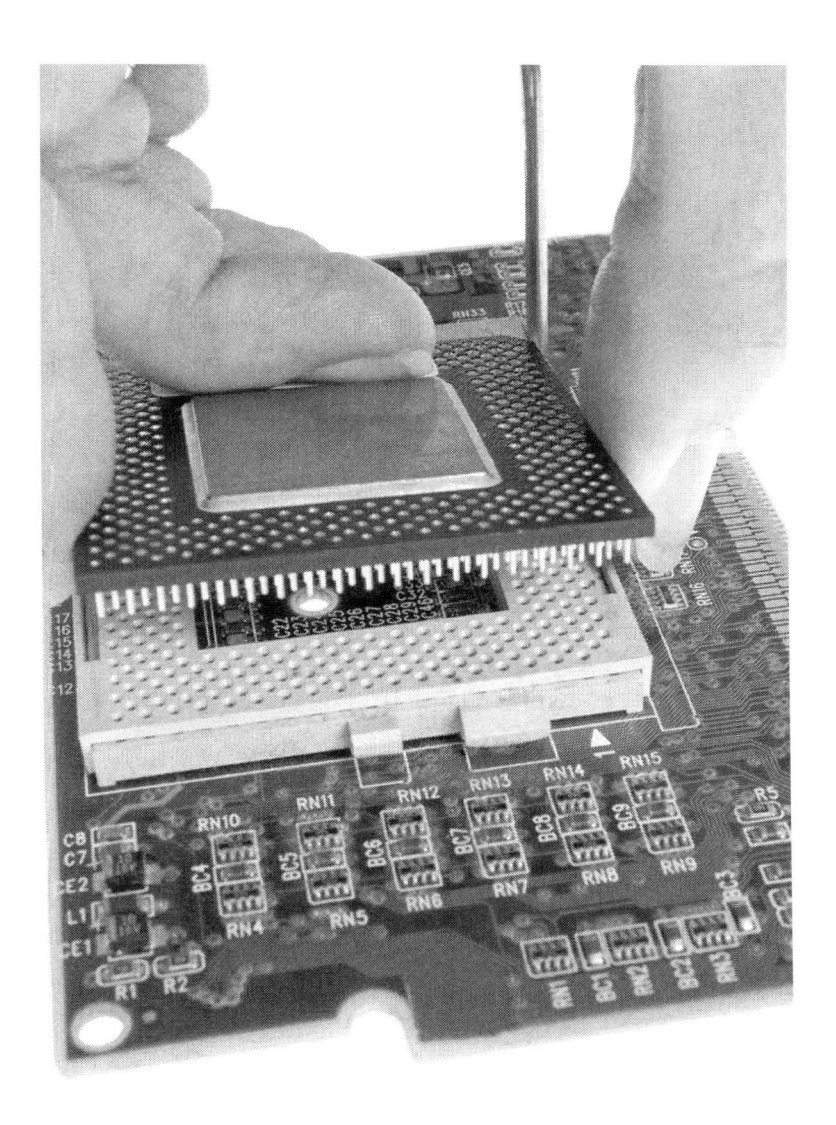

The processor is one of the most delicate and easily-damaged parts of the computer, as well as one of the more expensive ones, so you'll want to take care while installing it. None of this should require any hard efforts or feats of strength. If you find that you're having to strain to get something to click and fasten, that's a sign that it's not aligned correctly (either that or you have a misaligned processor and motherboard). If you find that happening, back up and try again from the first.

To install the processor:

1. Take it out of the box and look it over. In one corner, you should see a gold arrow.
2. Now find the processor socket on the motherboard. There should be a similar gold arrow in one corner of that.
3. Line up the two gold arrows. The processor goes into the motherboard's processor socket in that direction.
4. Some Intel motherboards have a cover over the processor socket that needs to be opened. All motherboards have a lever that needs to be lifted up.

5. With the lever up, insert the processor in the right orientation as determined by the gold arrows.
6. Close the lever to lock the processor into place.
7. Attach the cooler to the processor. How this is done depends on the type of processor. Intel processors have coolers have four attachment pins and all of them need to click shut. (This may take more than one try.) AMD coolers have side attachments that hook into the motherboard's square pegs, after which you pull a lever down to lock it into place.

Installing the RAM

After the difficult step of installing the processor, putting in the RAM is falling off a log easy. Find the RAM sockets on your motherboard. Pull down the two clips on the side of the socket. Line up the two notches (one in the socket, the other on the RAM stick). Press the RAM stick into place. This might take a little bit of muscle; don't worry, it's not that fragile (nor is it very expensive). When the RAM is seated correctly, the clips will snap back into place on their own.

Installing the PCI Cards

PCI cards include your video card (assuming you're not using the built-in on the motherboard) and may include other cards depending on what you're trying to build. Find the topmost slot that your video card can fit into. It should be matched up with a removable plate on the back of the case. (The plate is there to keep dust out in case you don't want to fill that slot.) Remove the plate. Slide in the PCI card so that its bracket (the thing you'll plug an attachment into, e.g. a connector for a monitor – you can't miss it) lines up where the plate used to be. That is, before you removed it, the plate was a part of the case; you should position the card so that its bracket now seems to be part of the case. This will position the card correctly so that you can now press down and seat it in the PCI slot of the motherboard. Screw the bracket into the case and you're done!

If you need to remove the card for any reason, look for a small lever on the back of the socket. In many cases you'll need to move this lever before removing the card.

Installing the Hard Drive

How hard drives are installed is the single feature in which cases vary the most, so you may want to refer to the manual that came with the case here. In general, though, there are two common ways to install a hard drive. Some cases have little drawers that you need to pull out, screw the hard drive into the drawer, and slide the drawer closed. With others, you just slide the hard drive into the bay and attach it with screws. It should be pretty self-evident which type of case you have, but again, check the manual if need be.

If you're installing multiple hard drives, it's a good idea to leave a little space between them if possible. Thus, if you have three hard drive bays and two drives, put them in the first and third rather than the first two or second and third.

Installing the Optical Drive

This is easy enough. Pull the cover off of the bay for the optical drive and slide it in. Attach with screws if necessary. (It may not be; some cases and optical drives just snap together.)

Installing the Power Supply

If your case came with a power supply and you're using that, you don't need to install it as it's already installed, in which case skip to the next section (Connect Everything). If you bought a separate power supply, it goes in the big rectangular hole in the back of the case, usually at the top (but in some cases it's at the bottom). You should mount it so that the plug is accessible through the hole in the case (obviously). Line up the screw holes on the power supply with those on the case, attach it with screws, and you're good to go.

At this point you have all of the goodies physically in place on your computer, but nothing works yet, because you haven't connected anything to the power supply. Thus, no electricity can be run through anything and that means your machine can't be turned on. Before you can use it, you need to connect everything together correctly with cables.

Connecting Everything

This is likely to be the most time-consuming and the hardest part of building your computer. If you chose a power supply with modular cables, you'll need to plug in each of the following:

- 24-pin motherboard cable
- 4-pin motherboard cable
- 6-pin PCI cable (for your video card if it has a socket for it)
- SATA power and data cables
- Front panel connectors
- Power switch and LED cables

24-Pin Motherboard Cable

Of all the cables for the power supply, this is the big honker. It's the main connection between the power supply and the motherboard, and it powers everything that doesn't have a separate connector of its own. If you're using a built-in power supply (or in some cases even a separate one), you may have a 20-pin and a 4-pin cable used together rather than a single 24-pin cable. Either way, plug them into the 24-pin socket on the motherboard, which is the longest socket it has so it's hard to make a mistake about it. Push the plug into the socket until it clicks and locks into place. This may take a bit of pushing to get it in all the way.

4-Pin Motherboard Cable

In addition to the big 24-pin socket, your motherboard should have a small 4-pin socket and there should be a matching cable coming from the power supply. Plug the latter into the former in the same way you did the 24-pin cable and socket.

6-Pin PCI Cables

As noted above, you'll use this only if you have a higher-end graphics card or other power-using card that goes in a PCI cable. The cable for this from the power supply looks a lot like the 24-pin and 4-pin cables that plug into the motherboard, but it has 6 pins and is usually labeled "PCI." This does not plug into the motherboard but rather into the end of your graphics card. If your video card doesn't have a socket, you won't need this cable.

SATA Power and Data Cables

Your hard drive(s) and optical drive require *two* cables each. One is a power cable that connects to the power supply. The other is a data cable that connects to the motherboard. The power cable is a thin little black job. The data cable is a smallish red cable that should have come with your motherboard. Your drive has two plugs, a long one and a short one. Plug the power cable into the *long* plug. Plug the data cable into the *short* plug. The data cable in question have two plugs, one on each end, but the plugs on the drives are L-shaped and will only accept the correct plug end. The other end goes into the motherboard. The plug for it is conveniently labeled SATA on the motherboard. The power cable is already connected to the power supply so you don't need to worry about that.

Molex Power Cables

These nasty little critters connect to and power various things on the case that (mostly) don't connect to the motherboard – in most cases that means fans. Each case fan should have one of them, while the power supply should have a number of sockets for them. Plug each one into the power supply. Note that this requires some pushing in many cases, which is why we call these cables "nasty little critters." (Your own language may be somewhat more colorful.)

Most fans plug into the power supply, but some few – frequently this includes the cooling fan for the processor – plug into the motherboard instead. If your processor's cooling fan comes with a dangling cord at the end of which is a three-prong plug, this goes into the socket on the motherboard labeled "CPU_FAN" or "SYS_FAN."

Front Panel Connectors

Most cases have some jacks on the front for headphones and microphones, plus at least one USB port, plus a FireWire port. Small cables come from each of these and are to be plugged into the motherboard (not the power supply). The sockets on the motherboard are usually labeled: USB, HD AUDIO, and 1394 (the last being the FireWire socket).

Power Switch and LEDs

The last thing to connect is the computer's on-off switch, together with some indicator LEDs. The cables for this are usually labeled. Exactly where they plug into on the motherboard varies from build to build, so you'll need to check the motherboard manual to make sure about it. It's always an 8-pin socket, though, so by this time it shouldn't be too hard to find.

Just in case you didn't have enough cables to sort out and plug in, or enough ways to get confused, some motherboards also have a small speaker that plugs into an 8-pin socket. Check the box the motherboard came in to see if such a speaker exists, and if it does (or even if it doesn't), consult the manual for your motherboard to make sure you have the right socket for the switch and LEDs.

Cable Management

While you're plugging all of this stuff in, cables will be accumulating inside of your computer. It's important to keep these out of the way as much as possible, for several reasons. You want to be able to see what you're doing as you connect your computer and get it ready to run. You want to see what you're doing later on if you go to upgrade. You want to make sure the air flows freely so your computer stays cool when it's running. This is why built-in cable management features are a useful consideration when choosing a case (see above). Failing that, it's a good idea to use twist ties to bundle groups of cables into neat packages that can be tucked out of the way.

Which cables should be bundled together is specific to your case, but in terms of what connects to what it doesn't matter. If the cables are physically close together, they belong together in a bundle.

Troubleshooting

The next thing to do, once the computer is put together and all of the cables plugged in appropriately, it to power it up and give it a test boot-up. Note that this will not boot up all the way, as you have not yet installed the operating system. The point here is to make sure that everything is connected correctly.

Connect a monitor to your video card first. Then plug the power supply into a source of electricity and turn the machine on. In a reasonably short time, you should see something called the POST screen. It should look like a blank black screen with some text on it including the words "Main Processor" and some information about your processor, a read out on your memory (RAM) available, and a few other odds and ends.

If you get this screen, then all is well. (Note: from this screen, you can hit the DEL key to make changes in the BIOS. We'll get to that when we discuss installing the operating system.)

If your computer simply doesn't turn on at all, then something has been installed or connected incorrectly. Check the following:

1. Is the processor correctly seated?
2. Is the RAM all the way into the sockets?
3. Are all the cables plugged into the right sockets?

Go over the instructions above and double-check everything. At some point you should find the error and be able to correct it.

If the machine does turn on, but you get beeping noises or the POST screen shows error codes, then you will need to find your motherboard's BIOS manufacturer (it may be visible on the POST screen, or you can find it online). Then consult one of the following pages:

Beep codes for AMBIOS

Beep codes for AwardBIOS

Beep codes for PhoenixBIOS

It's possible that you have a defective piece of equipment, most likely the power supply, the motherboard, or the processor (as those are the only ones that could cause systemic failure by not working). In that case, of course you will need to replace the defective part with something that will work. However, check all the other possibilities first;

defective parts are not as common as errors in putting it all together, especially if it's your first time building a computer.

Once you have a functioning machine, you are ready to install the operating system.

Installing the Operating System

Installing an operating system requires doing a little editing of the BIOS first in most cases. After that, the OS needs to be installed and configured. We'll go into handling the BIOS first, and then we'll discuss installing Windows, as that is by far the most popular option. If you want to check out Linux as an alternative operating system, we recommend that you consult Lifehacker's Guide. Installing Linux requires partitioning your hard drive, which is a fairly tricky process and almost worth a book in itself.

Even if you've installed or upgraded Windows before, you should realize that installing a fresh OS on a new, custom machine involves a few extra steps compared to doing it on a pre-built machine.

Editing the BIOS

When you start your computer, it runs through a procedure to bring up the POST screen shown above. Pressing a key (usually DEL, but the screen will tell you if it's different) takes you into the setup procedure for your Basic Input/Output System – your BIOS. This is where you can configure some of the basic, rock-bottom aspects of your machine's behavior. Bring this up before going into the installation of your operating system.

The BIOS will vary depending on your motherboard choice.

The first thing to do is to check that everything is installed properly. The BIOS gives you some diagnostic tools for the purpose. There are three things you want to look at here.

Check the System Information page to make sure that the amount of RAM you have operational is the same amount you installed. (You know that at least some of your RAM is installed correctly or your machine wouldn't boot up at all.) Most likely this will appear on the System Information page. With some motherboards, though, you won't see a System Information page available. In that case, re-boot the machine and look on the POST screen itself and the RAM should be listed.

If the total RAM is less than the amount you installed, that probably means one or more sticks aren't seated properly. Turn off the computer, open it up and check your RAM sticks to ensure they are all seated properly. Then re-boot and check again. If you're still short of RAM, that means one or more sticks are probably defective.

Next, check out the SATA configuration option. This should be configured as AHCI. That's the correct configuration for any version of Windows more recent than XP. (As of the date of this writing, you'll almost certainly want Windows 10, the latest version, or else Windows 8 or 7. Windows 7 is the most advanced version of the older-style Windows OS and many users still prefer it, but versions 8 and 10 are more advanced and considered better.)

The last thing you want to check is the Boot Priority or Boot Order page. What this does is to set up where the computer looks for stored programs. You want it to look at the optical drive first, then the hard drive. (If you're going to install Windows from a flash drive, make the USB port the first choice or anyway make sure it comes before the hard drive.) This is not so important for the first installation, because you don't have an OS on your hard drive anyway, but it will be very important for updates later on.

Of course, you also want to make sure that both drives are detected. If they're not, most likely they're not connected correctly, so turn off the computer and double-check that. The other possibility is that you have a bad drive. Better to discover that early, while the warranty is still in effect, right?

There are a lot of other things going on in the BIOS besides these three things, although they're the most important ones to look into before installing your operating system. How To Geek has a good in-depth exploration of the BIOS possibilities. (This is also a good website in general if you want more information on building your own computer, or on upgrading, creating a network, and so on. It's a little old, but the information is still good.)

Installing Windows

You should already have correlated your computer parts with your operating system options, but just in case, make sure you have the right version of Windows for your machine. Windows 10, 8 and 7 all come in two versions: 32-bit and 64-bit. If you have more than 4 GB of RAM installed, you need the 64-bit version. Otherwise it won't recognize and use all of your RAM.

Put the disc or flash drive in the appropriate receptacle and reboot your computer. If you've configured your BIOS properly, the computer should zip right over to the proper drive after displaying the POST screen briefly and load Windows from the disc or flash drive. You may at some point get a "hit a key to continue" type message. If that happens, well, hit a key. Gently, of course.

The program on your disc or flash drive will load an installer and you will then be taken to the install confirmation screen. The appearance is a little different between these three versions of Windows, but functionally they're the same.

Click the "Install Now" button. You'll be presented with the terms of use. Accept these (read them first if you want). Choose the "Custom (advanced)" option from the menu of choices for what kind of installation you want.

If you have more than one hard drive, select as the destination your primary hard drive (the first hard drive listed in your boot order when you were configuring the BIOS). Choose the "unallocated space" partition. Click Next. Windows will begin installing.

This is likely to take a while even if you have a very fast machine. Just kick back, break for lunch or something, and give it time. Microsoft operating systems are notorious space hogs, so there are a lot of files to read off the disc or flash drive and copy to your hard drive. After it's finished doing its thing, your computer will go ahead and boot up Windows automatically. If you have your speakers hooked up, you'll hear the Windows start-up chime and you'll see the familiar sequence of screens that eventually take you to the desktop (with Windows 7) or the Start screen (with Windows 8 or 10), and from there you're ready to use your computer.

Well, almost ready. There is a bit more to do yet, that you wouldn't have to do with a pre-made machine. This involves configuring Windows the way you want it, and especially installing your device drivers.

For further reading you can check out the links below:

How to Install Windows 10

How to Install Windows 8

How to Install Windows 7

Installing Your Drivers
The first driver you need to install is for your network connection that will allow you to access the internet. This will allow you to download all the

other drivers you need. Most likely, you'll have a wireless connection of some kind, but whatever you have it needs a driver unless your hardware works right out of the box. If not, you should have a CD that came with your motherboard and this will have the drivers for your network connection hardware.

Put that CD in the optical drive and find the Ethernet or Wi-Fi drivers you need. Don't install any of the other provided drivers just yet. You can probably find more up to date ones online.

Once you have access to the internet, the next step is to let Windows auto-install your drivers for you. This may catch everything, but chances are it won't. The next step, then, is to find drivers for any devices that need updating. You can do this from the Device Manager, which is accessed in Windows 7 from the Start menu, in Windows 8 from the Charms menu, and in Windows 10 click the search icon at the bottom left and type "device manager".

The Device Manager will list all of your devices (monitor, printers, mouse, keyboard, sound, etc.) and provide information about them. Anything that has a question mark or an exclamation point next to it has a problem with the driver of some kind. Usually, the Device Manager will tell you what driver is needed and you can then go online to the motherboard manufacturer's website. Your motherboard manufacturer will have a technical support page that lets you download the most recent driver for its device. There's one exception to this. If it's your video card that's missing a driver, go to the website for NVIDIA or AMD instead of your motherboard manufacturer's website. Downloading the driver will install it automatically.

Occasionally, the Device Manager may show you an "unknown device." In that case, you'll need to go on a hunting expedition using the CD that came with the motherboard. Insert this into the optical drive and browse it, checking the list of drivers against the Device Manager's list of devices. When you find drivers that are not reflected in the Device Manager's list, make a note of them. After that, you can go to the manufacturer's website for your motherboard and install the latest version. It may take a bit of fiddling about, but eventually you should be able to get all the drivers for your devices installed.

Installing Updates

The last step before you can actually *use* your new computer is to get Windows updated. You may have already started getting those pesky notices from Microsoft about this. If not, or if you prefer not to get those pesky notices and have turned off the auto-updating business, you can update Windows manually by doing one of the following:

- In Windows 7, go to the Start menu and mouse over All Programs, then choose Windows Updates from the pop-up menu.
- In Windows 8, go to the Charms menu, choose Settings, then Change PC Settings, then Windows Update, then Check for updates now.
- In Windows 10, click the Windows icon at the bottom left, then the settings icon, then go to "Update & Security" and check for updates.

Either procedure will take you online to the Microsoft website and a list of updates. You can choose all of them (which we recommend) or just some of them.

Once all of that is done, your new computer will be ready to use! All that's left is to install the software applications you want. That's really outside the scope of this little e-book, so we'll just say: congratulations!

More Resources

The state of the art in the field of computers advances at an incredible speed. (We know a guy who has a theory that an artificial intelligence from a possible future is guiding progress in the industry to midwife its own birth. But he's weird. We hope.)

While the basic information provided in this e-book is likely to remain valid for a while, and all of the information here is current at the time of this writing, it's most improbable that we've got the latest scoop on hardware and software available down to the last detail as of the time you read it. Here are some handy websites that will let you do some up-to-the-minute research before you actually shell out money for computer parts.

A great price comparison site is PC Parts Picker. It lets you comparison shop all sorts of computer hardware and also try out different builds for parts compatibility.

Tom's Hardware is a great site for reviews of computer hardware and also for news of the latest and greatest.

Extreme Tech is another fine hardware review site. Check both this and Tom's before making a final decision on anything important.

Logical Increments offers a PC Buying Guide that's game-oriented (which may be perfect for you and in any case puts a lot of pressure on any machine). Worth checking out if you want to build a high-end computer especially in terms of graphics.

Conclusion

Once you've finished building your new computer and installing your software, take a quick inventory of your feelings. Is that pride? A sense of accomplishment? Relief?

You've got a computer that is custom-designed for exactly what you want it to do. Not only that, but you've learned a lot in the process of putting it together. You've learned what parts go into a computer, how to shop for them and select them, how to install the bits and parts into a case, how to connect it all together, and how to install your operating system and get everything ready for use. Fantastic!

And useful, too, because one of the best things about a desktop computer is that it is *modular*. Want more RAM? A boost to your graphics capability? A bigger or faster hard drive? You can have that. All you need is to buy the right parts and replace what you originally put into your machine with something new. The skills you gained building your machine will enable you to do that, and they also work with pre-made machines should you feel like upgrading your old spare dinosaur.

One more time: congratulations! You've earned it and you deserve it.